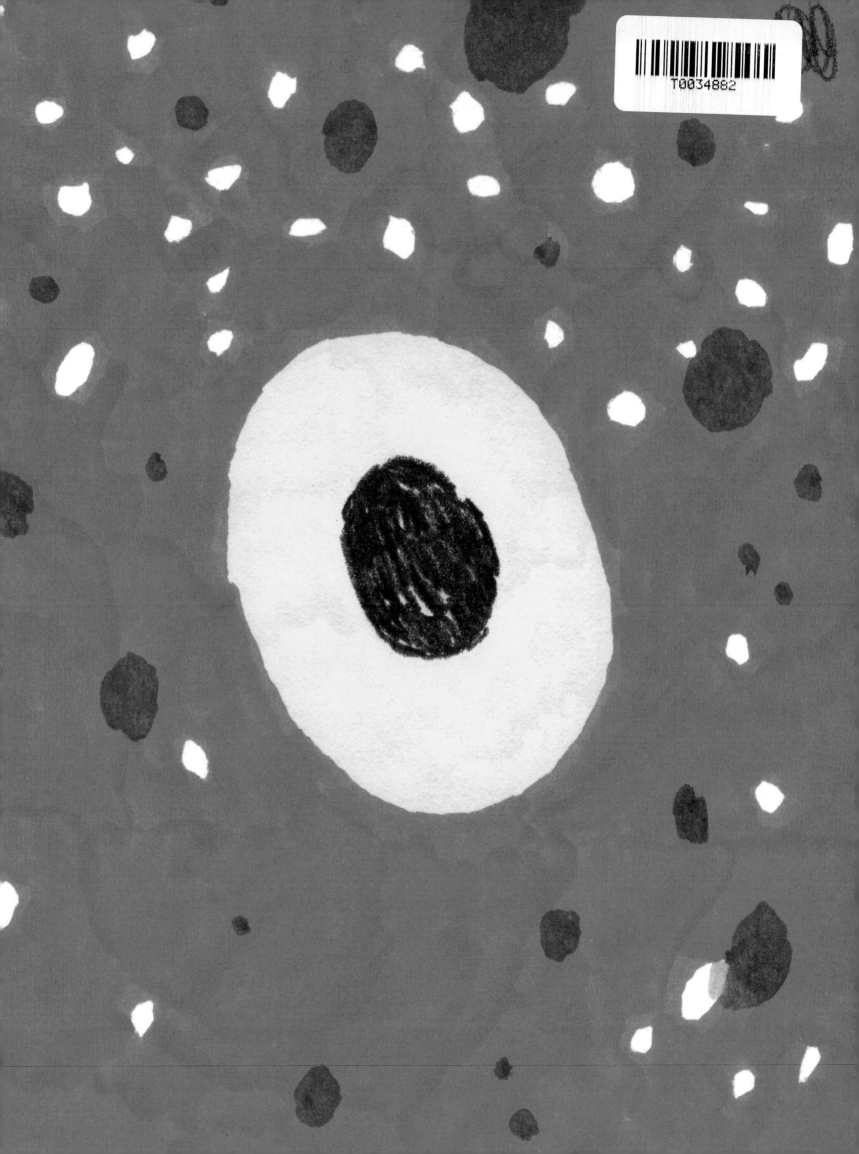

T0034882

OCTOPUSES
HAVE ZERO BONES

ANNE RICHARDSON

ILLUSTRATED BY ANDREA ANTINORI

 tra.publishing

ZERO, all by itself, is nothing.

Can you imagine nothing?

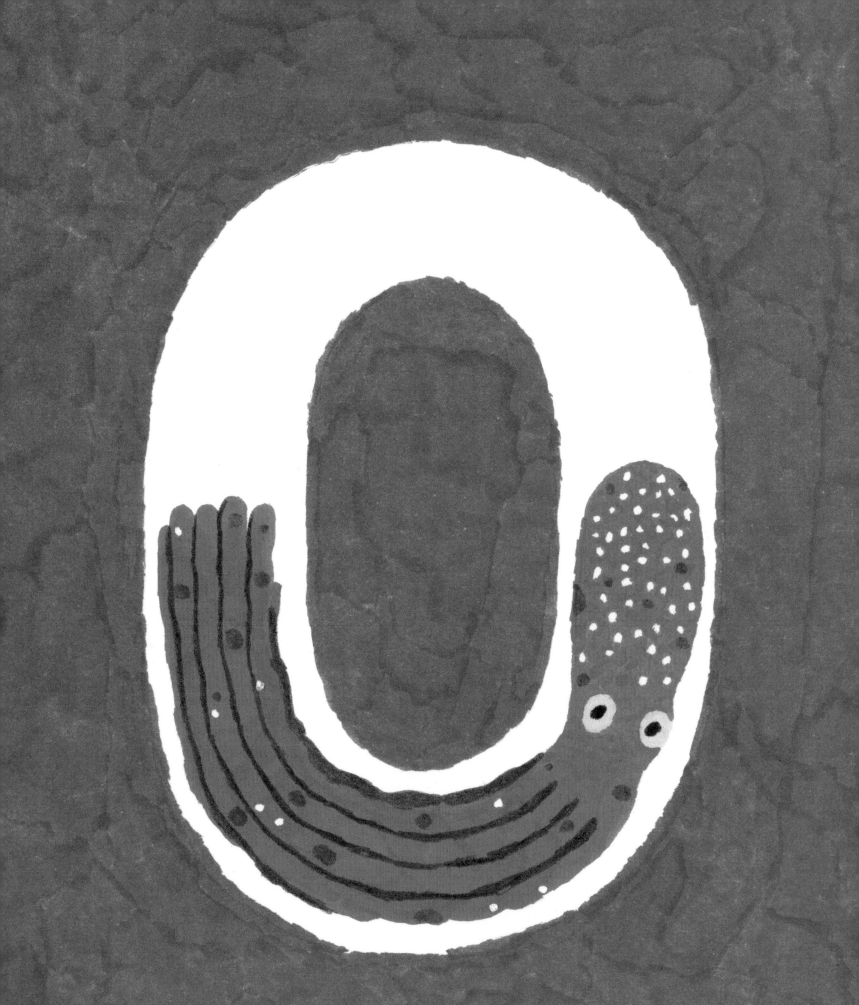

Octopuses have ZERO bones.
With no bones, octopuses can squeeze through very small spaces.

Dry Valleys, Antarctica, gets ZERO rain or snow.
In this driest spot on Earth, there's been
no precipitation for two million years.

Green hairstreak butterflies have ZERO green pigment in their wings. Instead of pigment, nanostructures called gyroids in the scales of the butterfly wings bend and scatter green light.

Tillandsia plant

Tillandsia plants need ZERO soil to grow.
These epiphytic plants get their water
and nutrients from the air instead.

For two weeks of winter in Longyearbyen, Norway, there is ZERO daylight. And in summer, there is twenty-four-hour sunlight.

But ZERO is not only nothing.
It's also a powerful digit. If we place a zero after
a whole number, it makes that number ten times bigger.
This is called powers of ten.

1
one

1
ten

1
one hundred

1,
one thousand

1,
ten thousand

1
one hundred thousand

1,
one million

1
ten million

1
one hundred million

1,
one billion

1

Of the one billion trillion stars in the universe,
there is ONE star in our solar system.
We call it the sun.

There is ONE heart in your body.

An octopus has three hearts!

An avocado contains ONE seed.

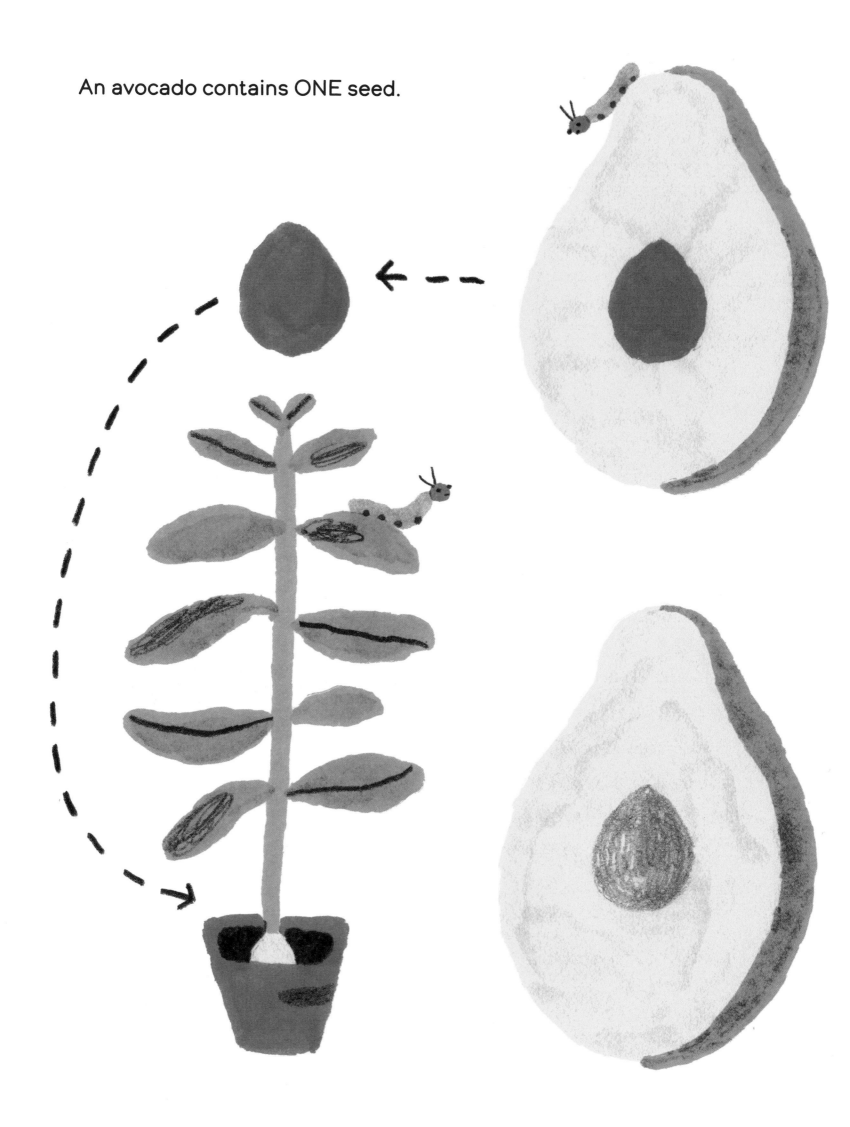

If we place a zero after the one, it makes the one ten times bigger.

The sound of your breath is TEN decibels—it is one of the softest sounds we can hear.

A helicopter sounds one thousand times louder than a falling feather. Each time you go up ten decibels, the sound becomes twice as loud.

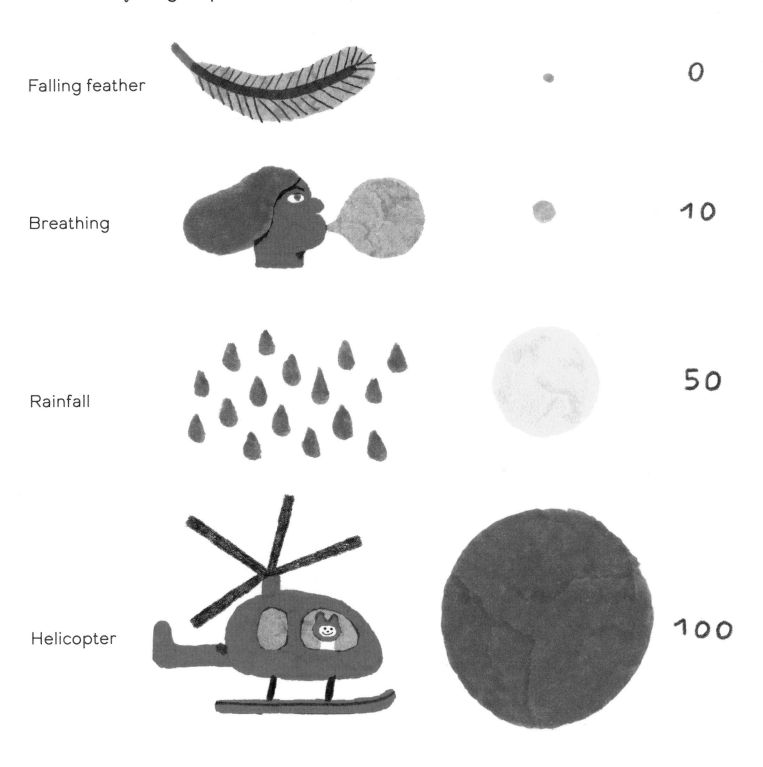

Falling feather   0

Breathing   10

Rainfall   50

Helicopter   100

Hermit crabs have TEN legs.

The front legs have claws for digging and gathering food.

These legs are used for walking.

Four of the legs are inside the shell.

1

2

4

6

10

Most people have TEN fingers.

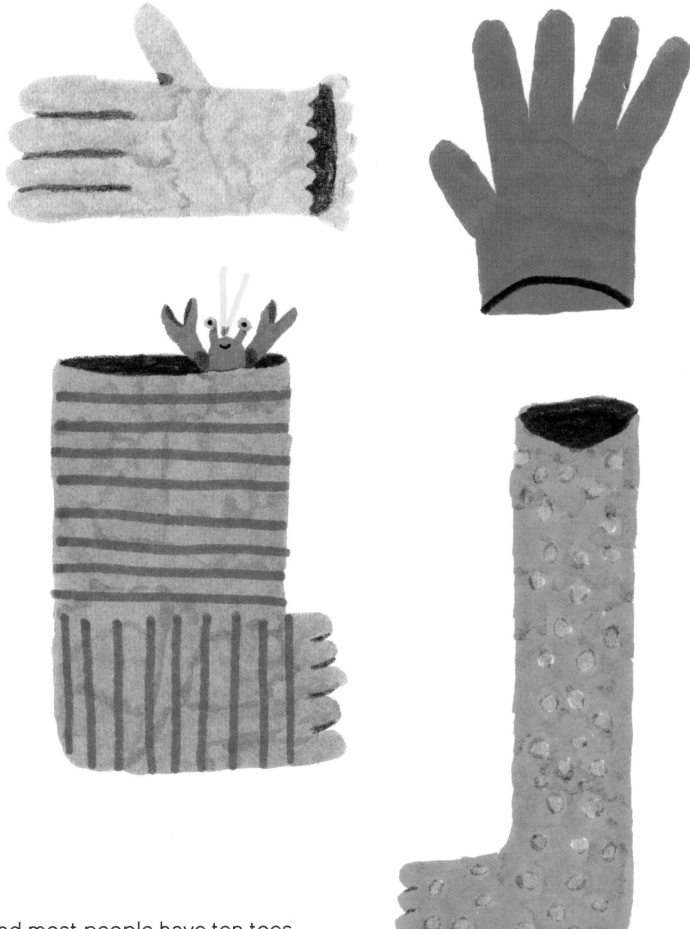

And most people have ten toes.

2

Peanut shells usually have TWO "nuts" inside.
Peanuts are legumes that grow underground.

10 BEANS

5 BEANS

2 NUTS

Peanut   Soybean   Fava bean

Soybean pods have up to five beans.
Fava bean pods have up to ten beans.

Mars has TWO moons.

PHOBOS

MARS

DEIMOS

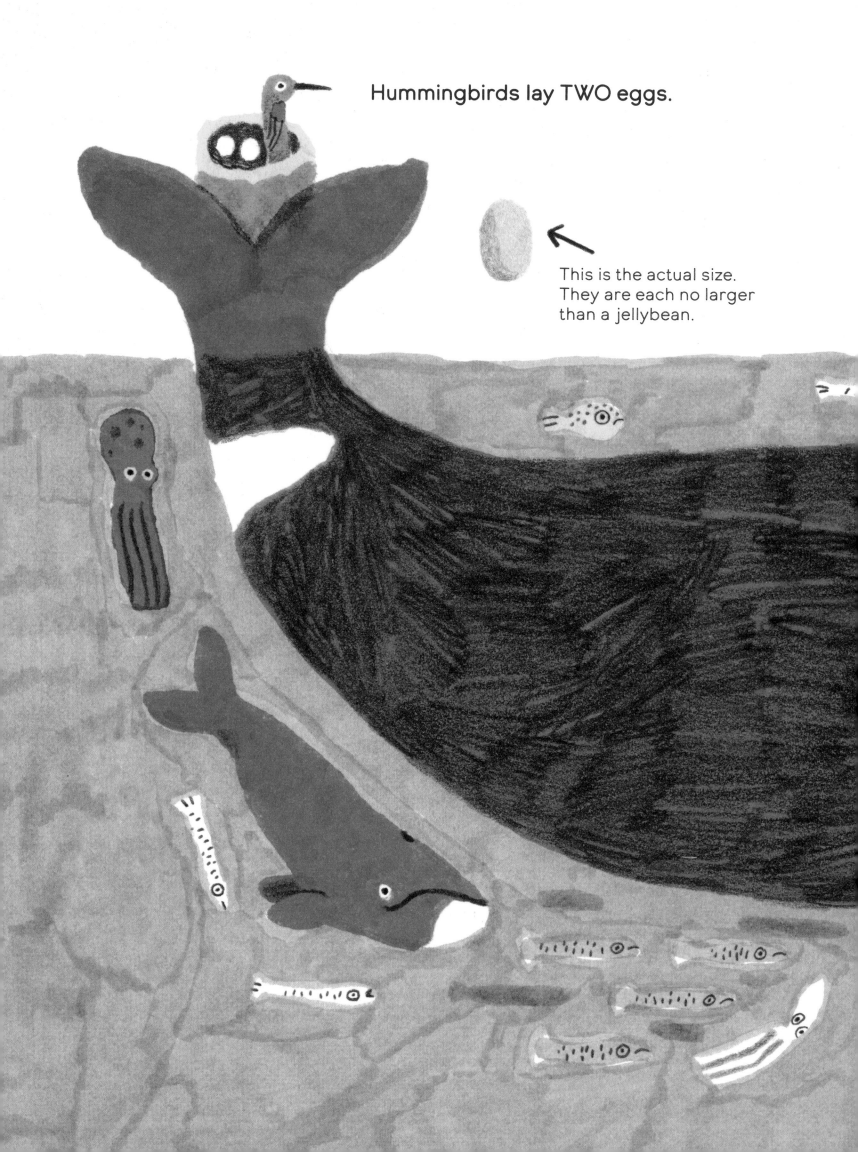

Hummingbirds lay TWO eggs.

This is the actual size.
They are each no larger
than a jellybean.

200

Now let's try placing two zeros after the TWO.

Bowhead whales can live more than
TWO HUNDRED years.
The bodies of these large animals are made up of
one thousand times more cells than human bodies.

There are more than TWO HUNDRED different languages spoken in Los Angeles, California.
Here are the words for "hello" in fourteen of them.

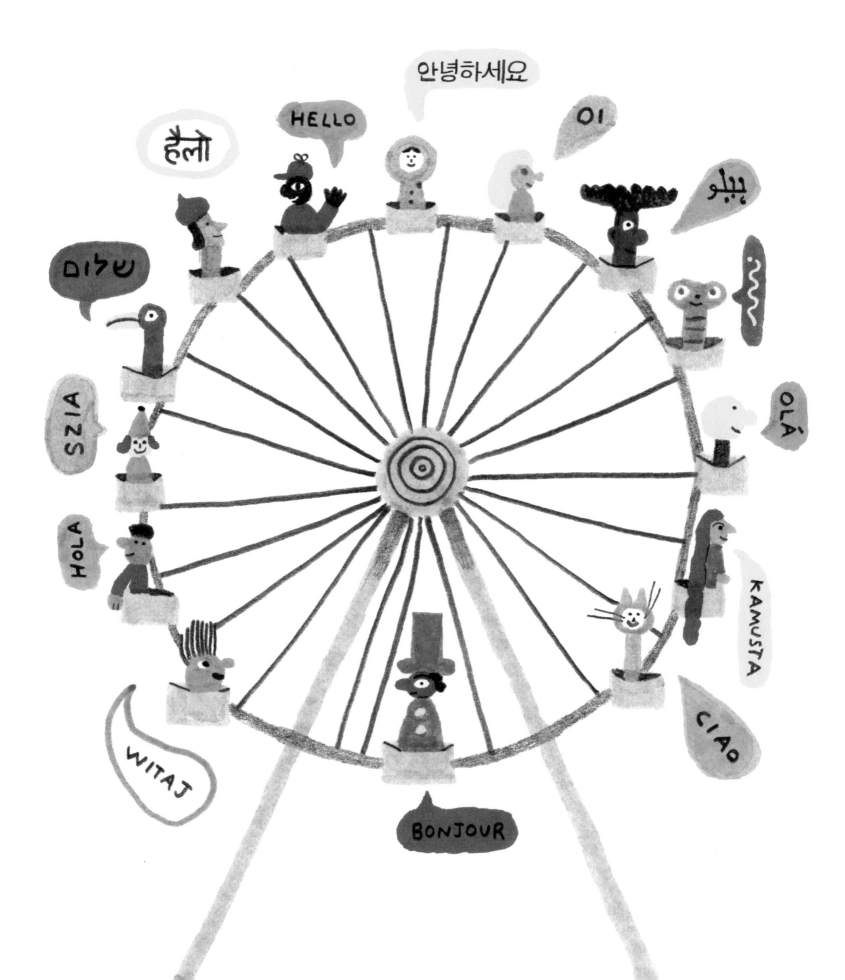

There are TWO HUNDRED types of cells in the human body.
There are about thirty trillion total cells in our bodies.

Trillium flowers have THREE petals.

6 STAMENS

3 SEPALS

3 PETALS

3

Sloths have THREE toes on each foot.
Three-toed sloths have three fingers on each hand
and two-toed sloths have two fingers on each hand.
All sloths have three toes on each foot.

It takes an average of THREE days
for food to pass through your
digestive system.
Even though they are much larger
than we are, elephants take only
one day to digest their food.

3,000

When you put three zeros after the three, that number is three thousand.

6000 m

Cirrus clouds are as high as six thousand meters!

CIRRUS

ALTOSTRATUS

ALTOCUMULUS

3000m

2000m

Some cumulus clouds can hang as low as two thousand meters.

CUMULUS

There are THREE THOUSAND meters between you and mid-height clouds.

A black bear's heart beats THREE THOUSAND times every hour during much of the year.

However, it beats much faster just before hibernation and then very slowly during hibernation.

There is a giant sequoia tree
in Yosemite National Park that is
THREE THOUSAND years old.

Its name is Grizzly Giant. This tree is 96 feet around
and 210 feet high!

4

The blue-gray gnatcatcher is FOUR inches long.

Your heart has FOUR chambers.

ATRIA

VENTRICLES

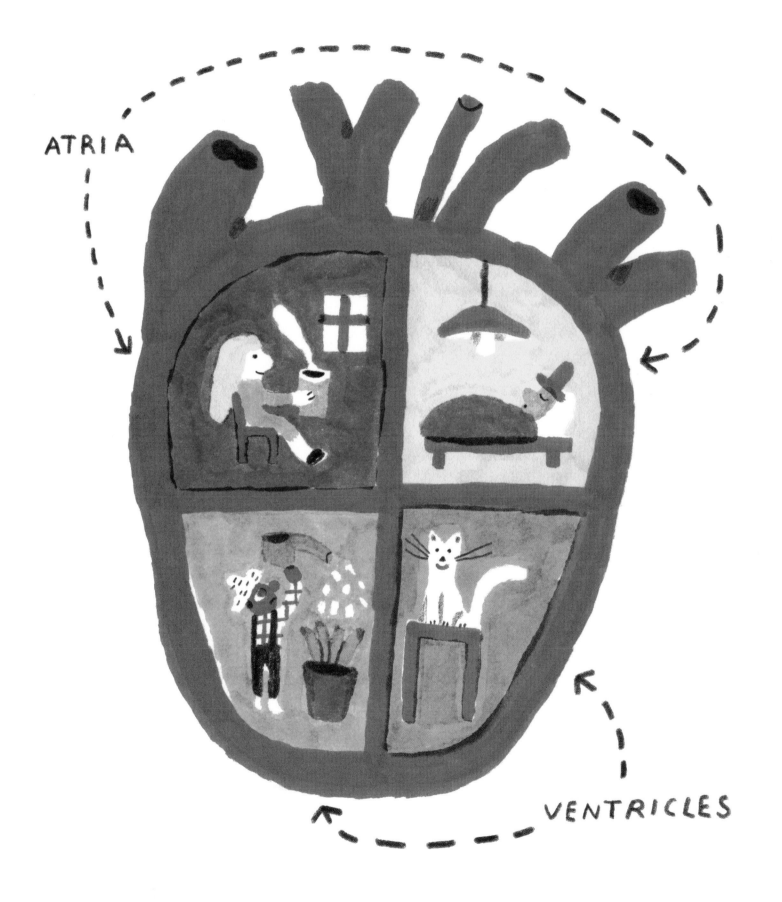

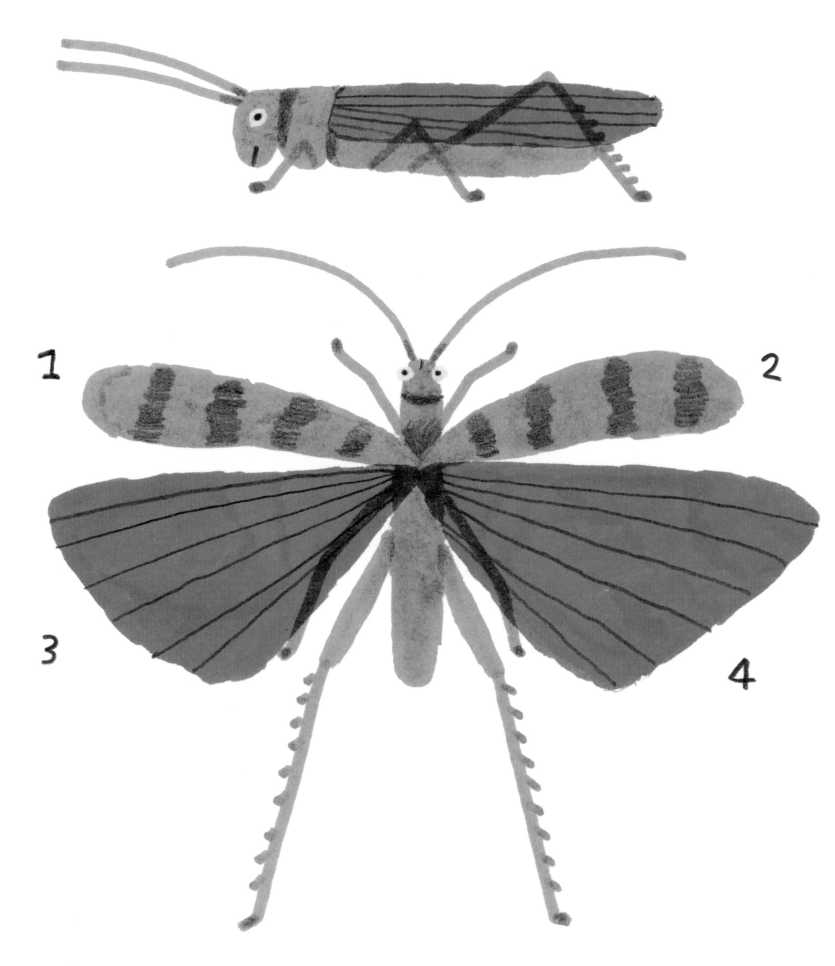

1

2

3

4

Grasshoppers have FOUR wings.
They are tucked away unless the grasshopper is jumping!

40,000

Now, let's multiply. Four times ten times ten times ten times ten is forty thousand.

There are FORTY THOUSAND words in a typical short novel.

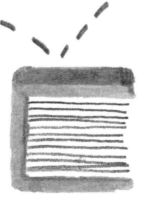

Alice's Adventures in Wonderland
This one has twenty-six thousand words (a very short novel).

Island of the Blue Dolphins
This one has forty thousand words (a short novel).

The Secret Garden
This one has ninety-one thousand words (a standard-length novel).

You take FORTY THOUSAND breaths each day.
You breathe air in and out through your lungs.
Grown-ups only take twenty thousand breaths each day.

There are FORTY THOUSAND grains in a two-pound bag of rice.

5

There are FIVE petaloids on a sand dollar.

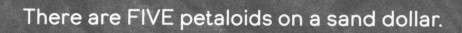

These little pores
are for breathing!

The Earth has FIVE ocean basins.

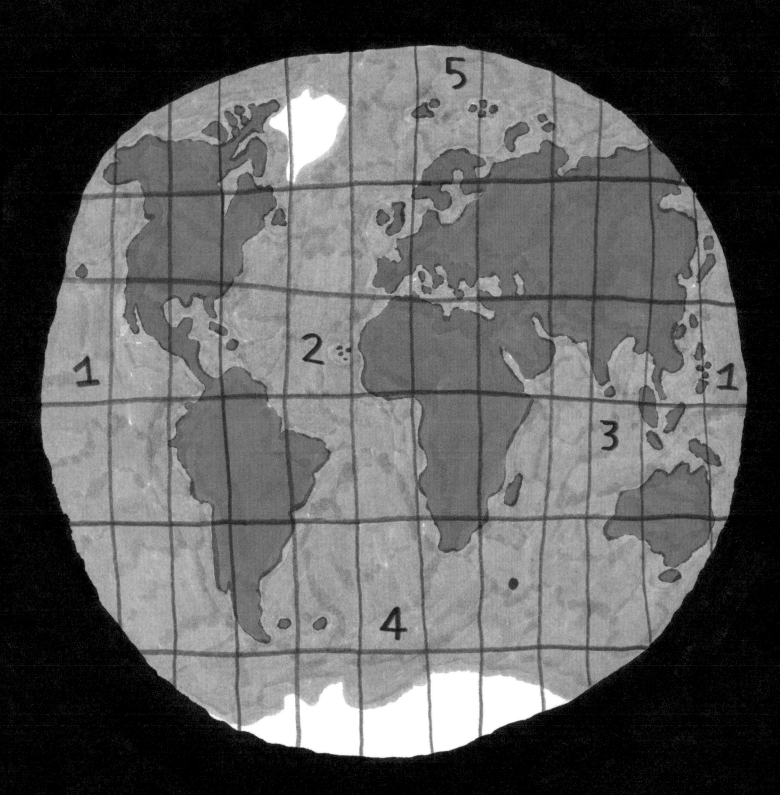

1 PACIFIC   2 ATLANTIC 3 INDIAN
4 SOUTHERN 5 ARCTIC

Apples contain FIVE seed chambers.
Each chamber may have one
to three seeds inside.

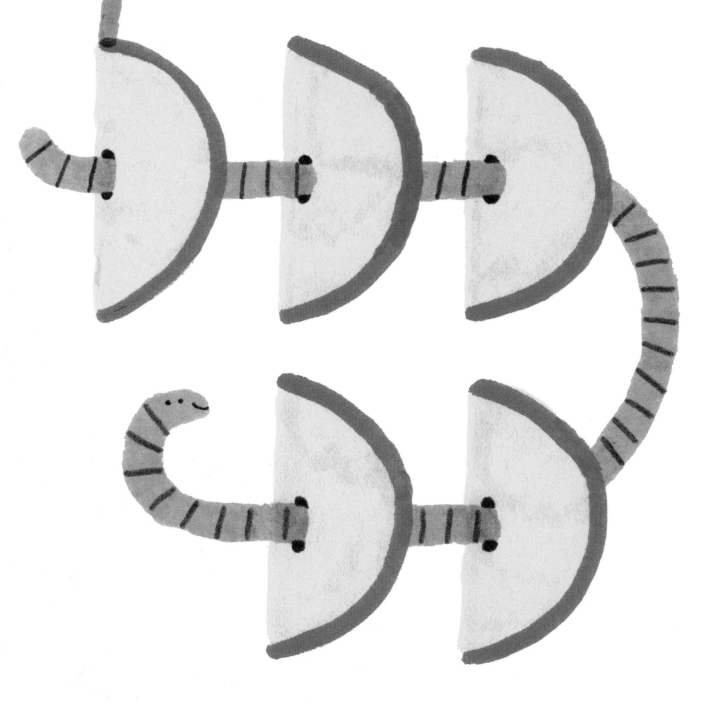

500,000

Five hundred thousand is half of one million; this is the number you get when you put five zeros after the five.

When you look up into the branches of a mature oak tree, you will see up to FIVE HUNDRED THOUSAND leaves.
There are six hundred species of oak.

SOUTHERN RED OAK

BUR OAK

CHINKAPIN OAK

NORTHERN PIN OAK

These are four types of oak trees that grow in Michigan.

A trip to the moon and back is FIVE HUNDRED THOUSAND miles.
The Earth's diameter is four times wider than the moon's diameter.
The distance between the Earth and moon is thirty times
the diameter of the Earth. (This drawing is not to scale!)

There are FIVE HUNDRED THOUSAND children's books
in the United States Library of Congress in Washington, D.C.

There are SIX strings on a guitar.
With six strings and twenty frets, a guitar
has a range of nearly four octaves!

A snowflake has SIX points.
To make a snowball, you'll need
about six million snowflakes.

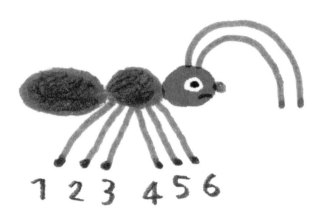

Ants have SIX legs.
All insects have six legs.

1 2 3 4 5 6

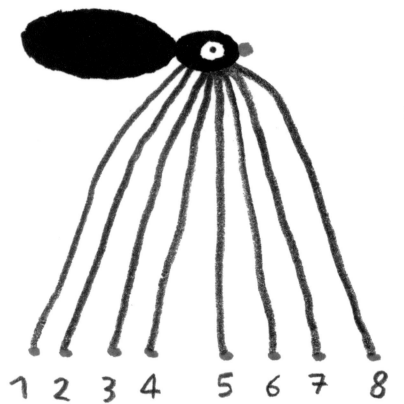

Spiders have eight legs.

1 2 3 4 5 6 7 8

Roly-pollies have fourteen legs!

1 2 3 4 5 6 7 8 9 10 11 12 13 14

6,000,000

Multiply six by one million and what do you get?

The sixth smallest state, Vermont, is SIX MILLION acres.
Six hundred thousand people live in Vermont.

The Amazon, Nile, and Missouri river systems are each SIX MILLION meters long, the same length as the radius of the Earth.

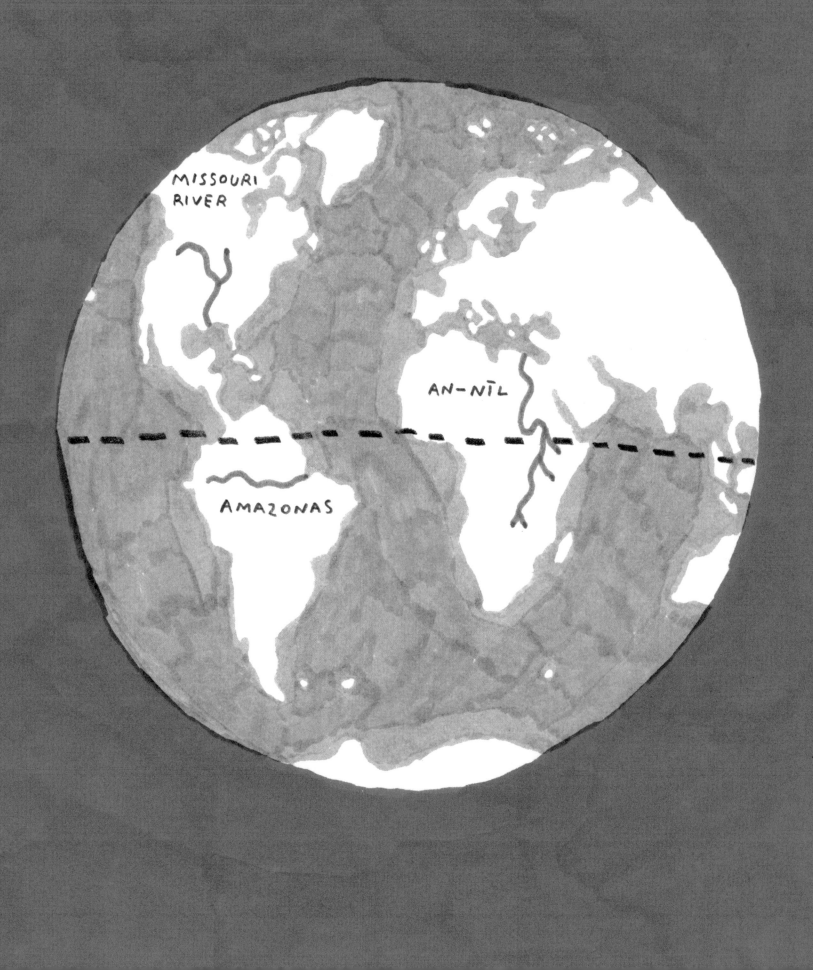

There are SIX MILLION people living in Singapore.
The Republic of Singapore is a sovereign island city-state,
and in size it is 178,000 acres.

The Mariana Trench is
the deepest point on Earth,
at SEVEN miles deep.
It's in the western
Pacific Ocean.

7

The continental shelf is at 500 feet.

Sunlight reaches the first 3,300 feet.

The abyssal zone starts at 13,000 feet.

The dumbo octopus has been
found at four miles deep.

The deepest point is seven miles.

The most seismically active part of the United States, Alaska, has a magnitude SEVEN earthquake every year.

Pure water has a pH of SEVEN.
This is neutral, neither acidic nor basic.

SEVENTY MILLION gallons of water fall over Niagara Falls every ninety seconds.

PH 7
Water

PH 2
Lemon

PH 6
Milk

Let's place seven zeros after the seven.

PH 9
Toothpaste

PH 12
Soap

70,000,000

SEVENTY MILLION years ago,
dinosaurs were in their final years.

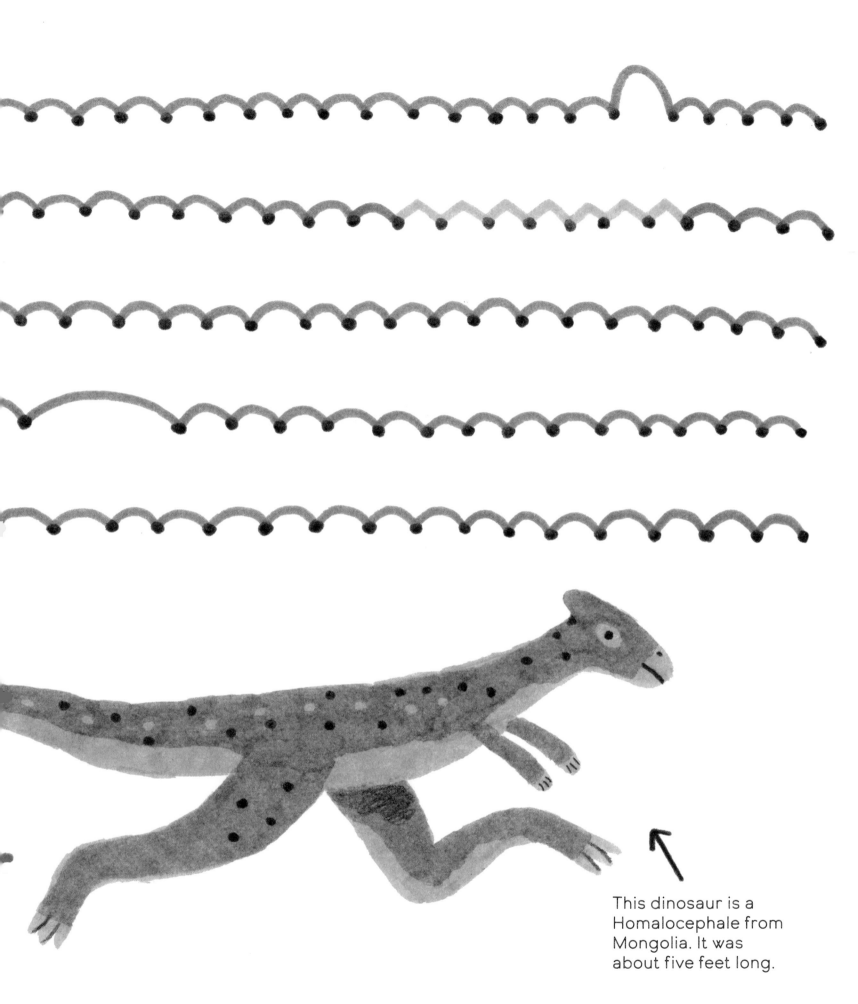

This dinosaur is a Homalocephale from Mongolia. It was about five feet long.

You will probably have walked SEVENTY MILLION steps by the time you reach adulthood.

Tardigrades (also called water bears) have EIGHT legs.
Water bears are nearly microscopic animals that live in moss and other wet places. They can survive in more extreme environments than most animals.

The highest note on a piano is called C8. The size of
the sound wave it produces is EIGHT centimeters long.
A standard piano has eighty-eight keys.

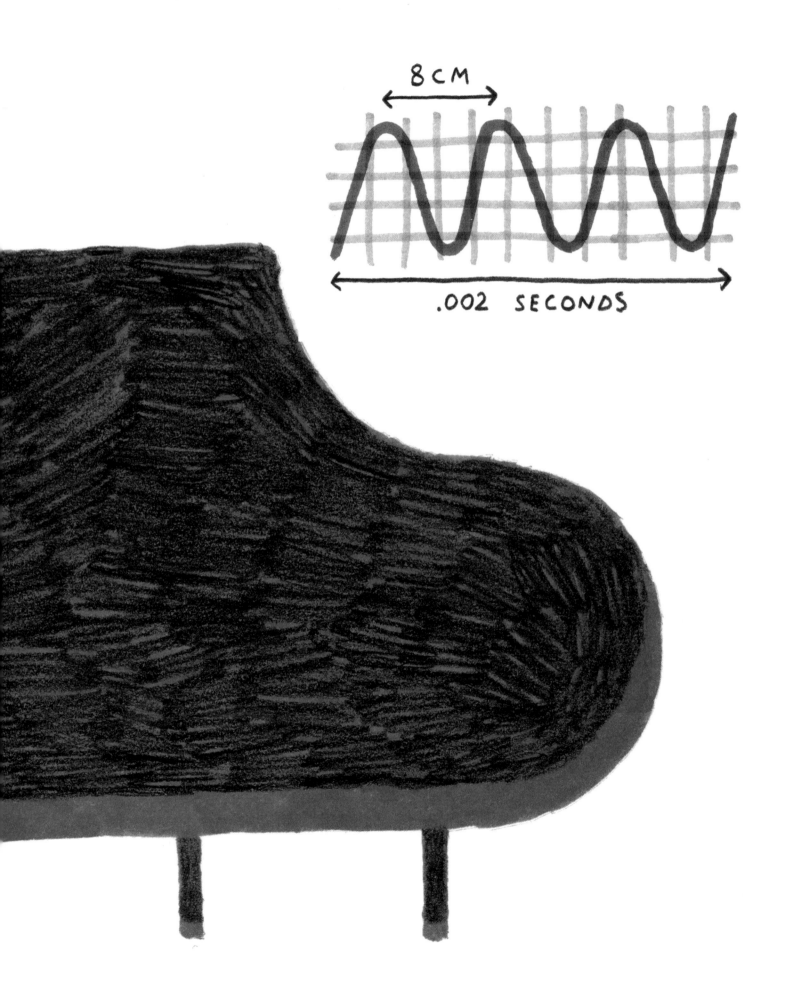

8 CM

.002 SECONDS

In most places, the largest raindrops
are EIGHT millimeters across.
When raindrops get larger than eight
millimeters, they usually split into
multiple drops on their way down.

Here's how
big the largest
raindrop can be!

800,000,000

Eight zeros after the eight is eight hundred million.

VOYAGER 1

0
1
2
3
4
5
6
7
8

Saturn is about EIGHT HUNDRED MILLION miles from Earth. **Voyager 1** took three years and two months to get to Saturn.

There are EIGHT HUNDRED million bacteria in a teaspoon of grassland soil.
There are between ten thousand and one hundred thousand different species of bacteria in a teaspoon of soil.

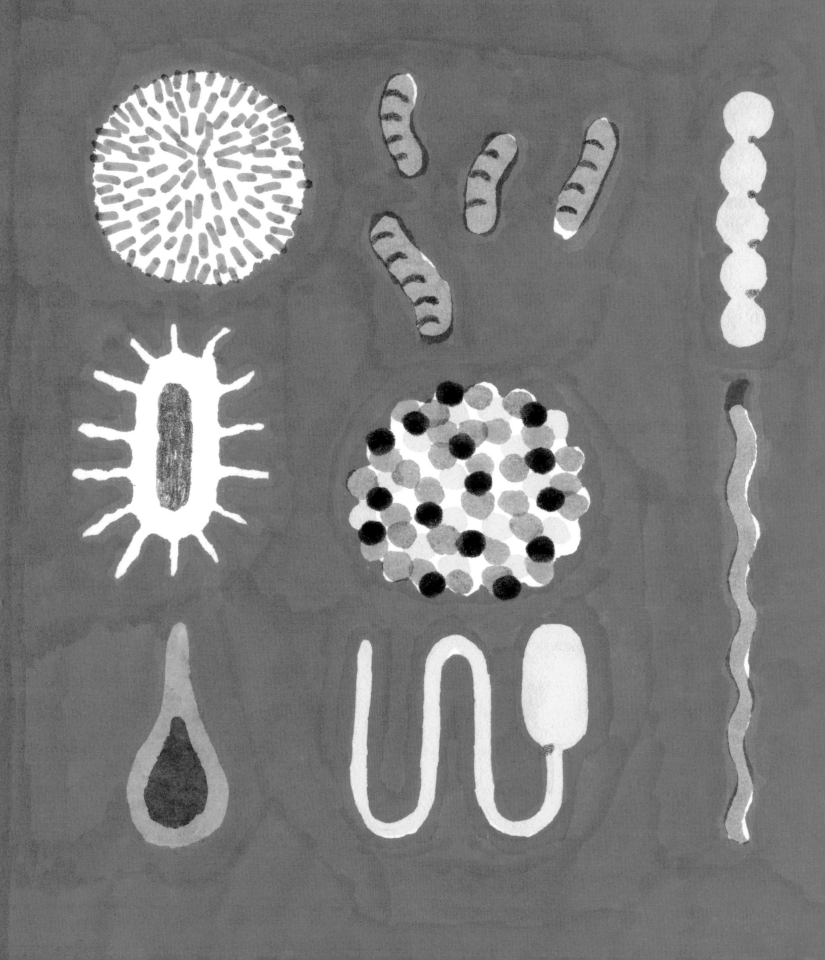

The first animals evolved EIGHT HUNDRED million years ago.
The first animals were sea sponges, and they still exist.
They don't have eyes or mouths and don't move around.
Sponges can be many different shapes, sizes, and colors.

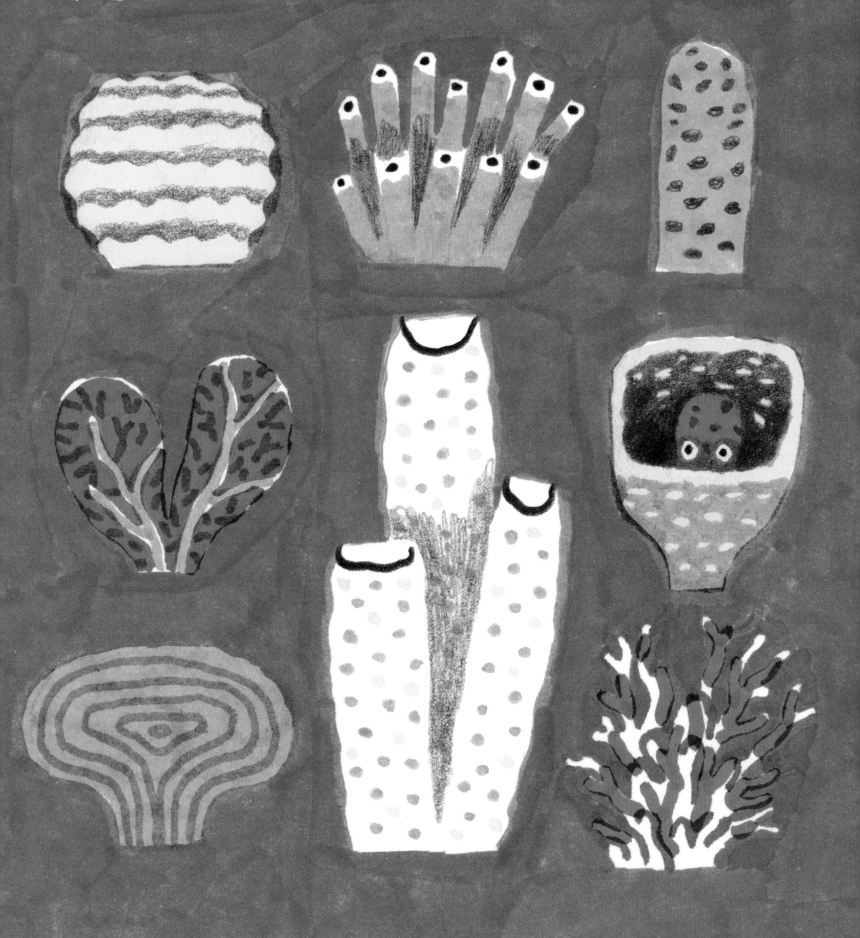

The NINE-spotted ladybug is the official state insect of New York.
Counting the number of spots on a ladybug is one way to tell what kind of ladybug it is. This ladybug was once common but is now a rare insect.

The element fluorine has NINE protons in the nucleus of its atoms.
The number of protons in an atom's nucleus determines the properties of the element. Protons are one of the smallest things in the universe. They are so small they cannot be seen under a microscope. Sodium fluoride in toothpaste comes from fluorine.

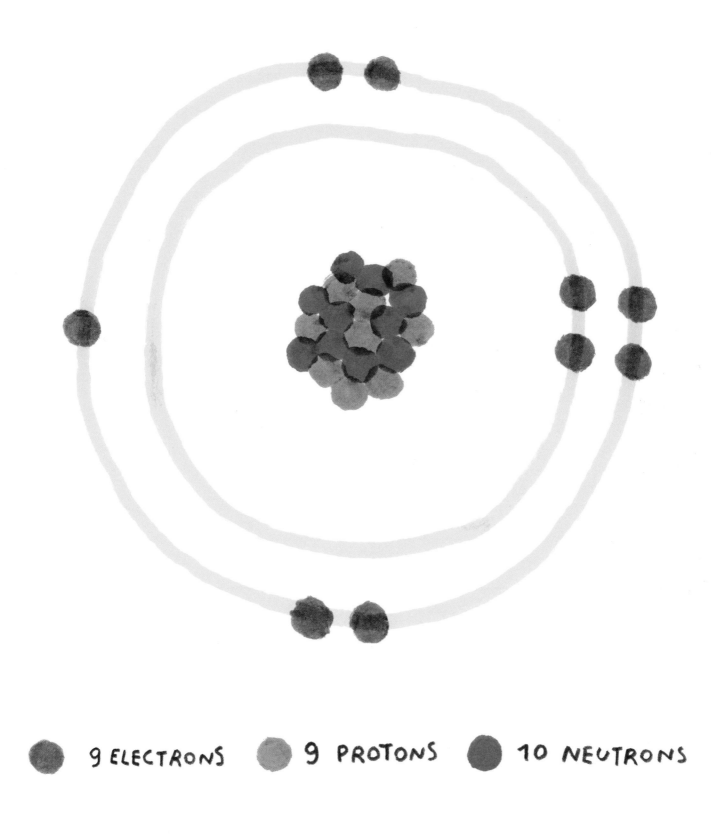

9 ELECTRONS   9 PROTONS   10 NEUTRONS

← 9 FEET

A narwhal's tusk can be NINE feet long.
The very sensitive tusk helps narwhals detect the
surrounding water temperature, pressure, and salinity.

9,000,000,000

Placing nine zeros after the nine is a very large number!

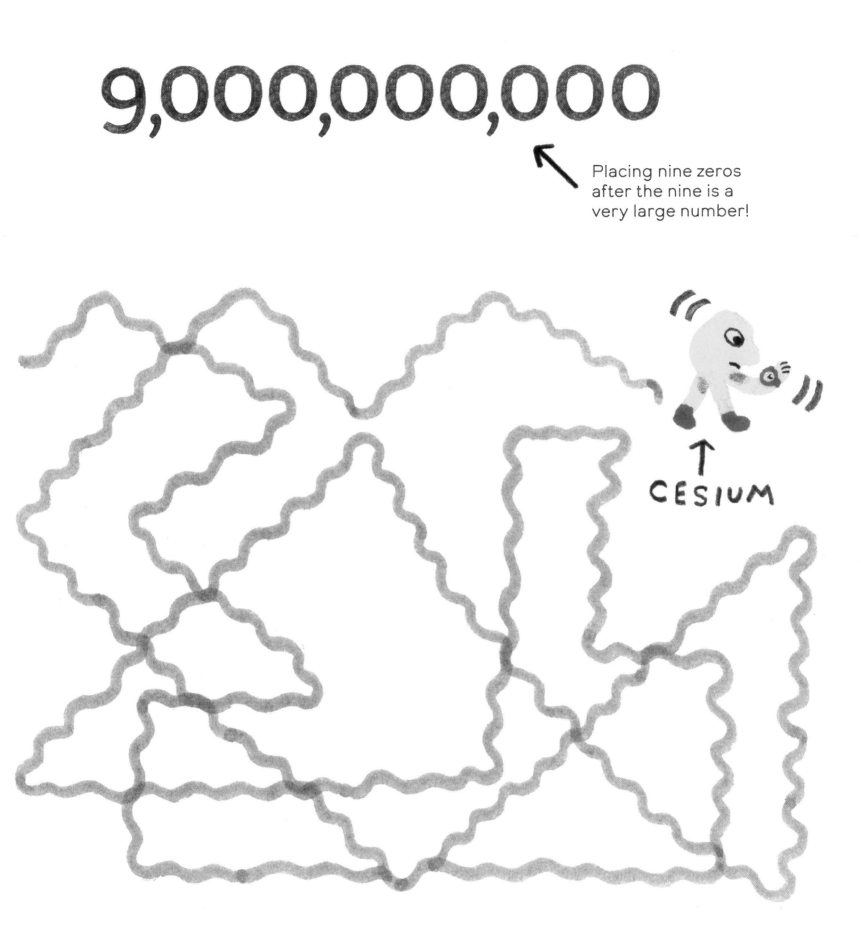

CESIUM

It takes one second for a cesium atom to jiggle NINE BILLION times. This is how we measure time! Measuring time with atoms is a relatively new idea—seconds were first defined based on solar and lunar time, and then later by the motion of pendulums.

The people of the United States eat a combined
total of NINE BILLION pounds of bananas each year.
That's eighty-one bananas per person.

NINE BILLION years went by after the Big Bang
before the sun and our solar system formed.

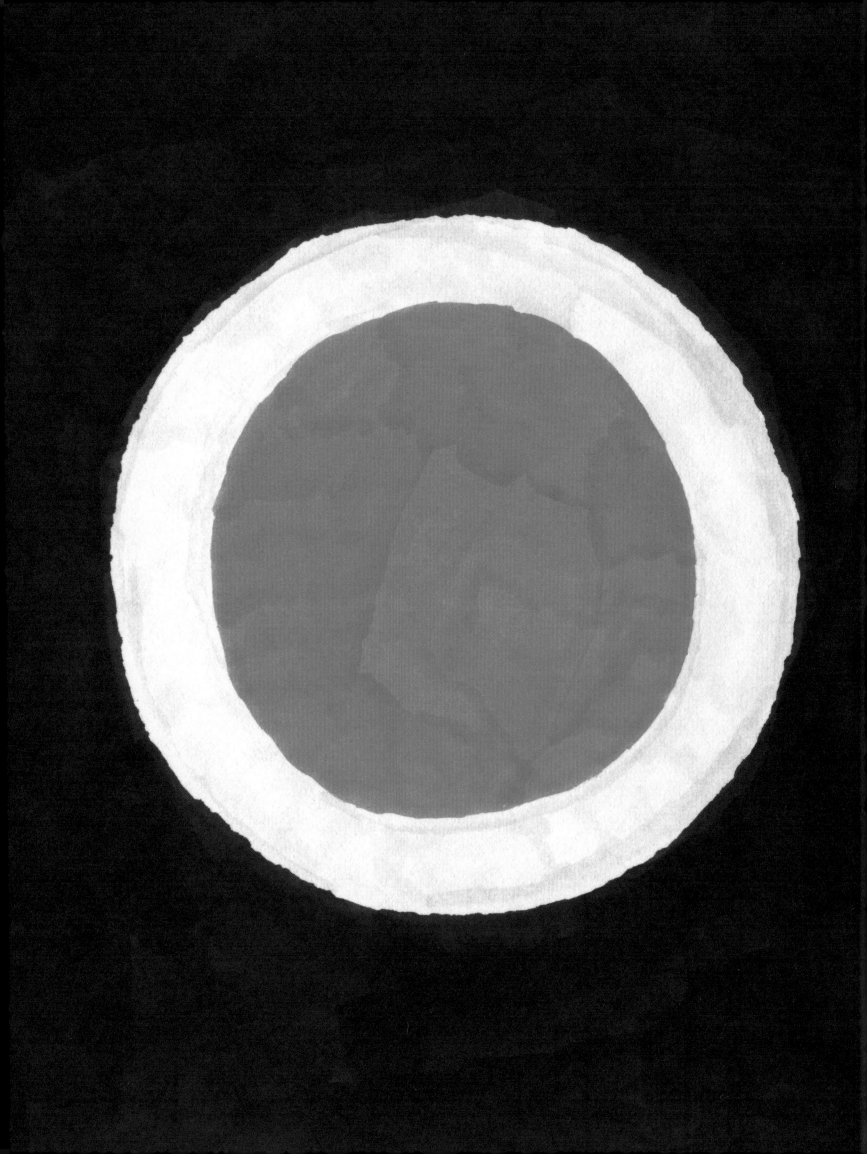

NINE BILLION is a big number, but it's not the biggest.
You can keep on counting forever. It takes light one year
to travel six trillion miles. Just imagine the distance
the sun's light may have traveled in its lifetime!

AUTHOR'S NOTE

One evening while I was writing this book, sixteen ants walked past my back door in one minute. I sat down on the deck and counted them as they passed by. Ants seem to be there all the time, streaming along in two directions. If they walk along that path the same way continuously, that would mean that approximately twenty-three thousand ants walk past my back door each day. That's a lot of ants!

I can't tell them apart, so I would not know whether it's twenty-three thousand individual ants or if a smaller group is making laps. And I haven't checked whether they're actually there at all times. I wonder how many steps they take each day...and whether it's more than I do.

According to biologist E. O. Wilson, there are over a quadrillion ants alive on Earth (that's more than the number of stars in our galaxy), and I wonder how many of them (ants, not stars) are in my backyard.

In the spring of 2020, my children and I began to count, measure, and wonder about the numbers associated with all kinds of things in the world. How many seeds are in an apple, how small are hummingbird eggs, and how many miles away is Saturn? We collected numbers and wrote them down. Over time, I organized the material and wrote this book.

I encourage you to go out into the world and count or measure something, anything. Can you count how many sounds you hear in one minute, or the number of cars that drive by in one hour? Can you find a way to measure the amount of rain that falls in one rain shower, or the number of bananas you eat each year? Do you ever wonder how big a cloud is or how long it takes an apple to grow?

Counting and measuring are wonderful ways to begin to get to know the world around us. Numbers, along with the units we count or measure, allow us to describe and compare how many, how far, how long, how loud, and so much more. This ability is useful to us as we try to understand the world, to interact with one another in society, and to find solutions to problems. It's also simply delightful to know how many points there are on a snowflake and to wonder how many it might take to make a snowball.

Go count or measure something, be astonished, take a closer look.

I hope you discover many wonderful things.

Anne Richardson, Author

Anne Richardson creates experiences that kindle your curiosity. In her work, everything in the world is astonishing and worthy of our attention, from a drop of rain to the way we figure things out together. She is the senior director of Global Collaborations at the Exploratorium, San Francisco, where she works with partners worldwide to imagine and create new science centers and other extraordinary learning experiences. Richardson holds a PhD and an MS in environmental studies from Antioch University New England, and a BA in art history from Northwestern University. She lives in the San Francisco Bay Area with her family, including two little explorers. This is her first children's book.

annerichardsonbooks.com

Andrea Antinori, Illustrator

Andrea Antinori is an award-winning illustrator based in Bologna, Italy. He has loved animals and loved to draw them since he was a kid. His favorite animal changes all the time. He likes octopuses very much. He also loves lemurs. He even wrote and illustrated a book called **The Lives of Lemurs**. Other books he has illustrated include **A Book About Whales** and **The Great Battle**, which has won major international awards. He studied graphic design and illustration at ISIA in Urbino and at Escola Massana in Barcelona.

andreantinori.com

For my two little ones, whom I love beyond measure.—A. R.

Octopuses Have Zero Bones:
A Counting Book About Our Amazing World

Author
Anne Richardson
Text copyright © 2022 Anne Richardson

Illustrator
Andrea Antinori
Illustrations copyright © 2022 Andrea Antinori

Publisher & Creative Director
Ilona Oppenheim

Art Director & Designer
Jefferson Quintana

Editor
Andrea Gollin

Fact Checker
Adam Dunlop-Farkas

Proofreader
Ileana Oroza

Printing
Printed and bound in China by
Shenzhen Reliance Printers

All rights reserved. No part of this publication may be reproduced or transmitted in
any form or by any means, electronic or mechanical, including photocopy, recording,
or any other information storage-and-retrieval system, without written permission
from Tra Publishing.

ISBN: 978-1-7353115-2-4
Third printing, April 2023

Octopuses Have Zero Bones: A Counting Book About Our Amazing World is printed on
Forest Stewardship Council certified paper from well-managed forests.

Tra Publishing is committed to sustainability in its materials and practices.

Tra Publishing
245 NE 37th Street
Miami, FL 33137

trapublishing.com

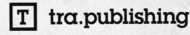

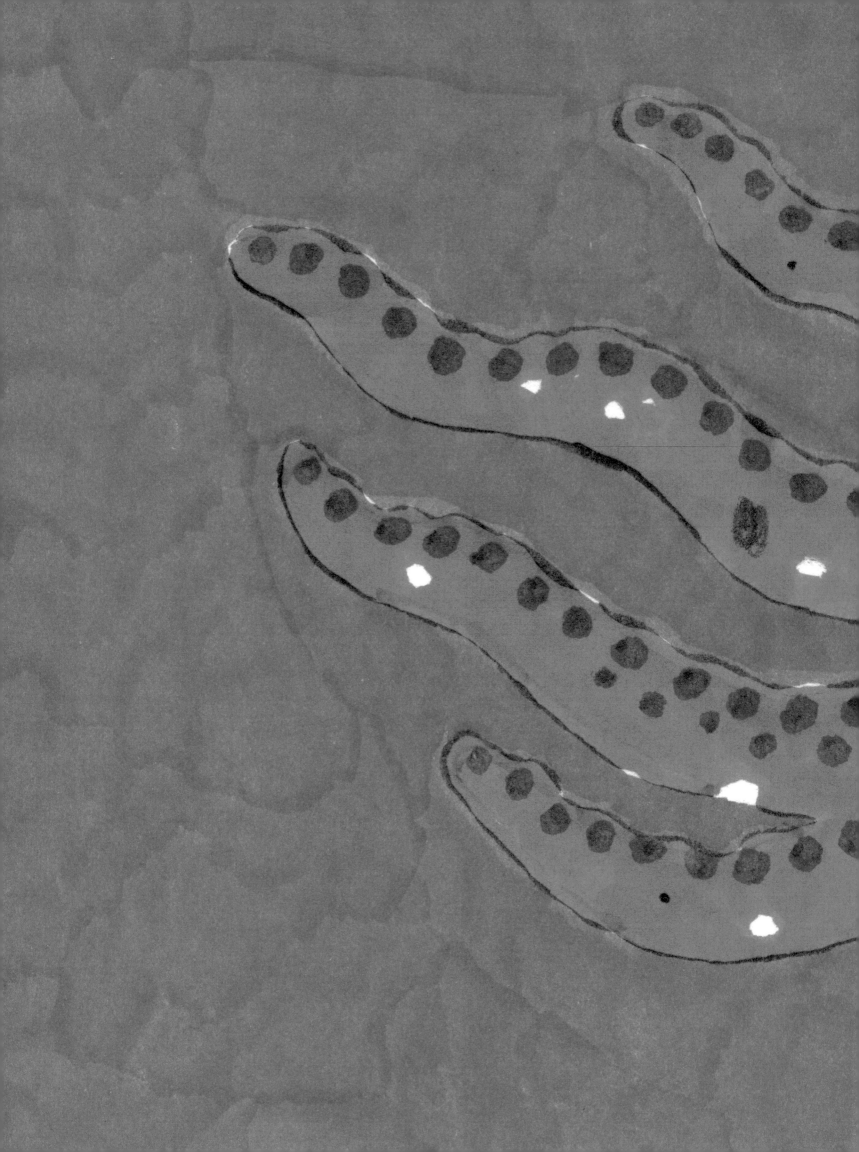